Old Llandudno and its Tramw

by Bernard Byrom

A view looking from Gloddaeth Avenue towards the seafront sometime around 1908. Behind the advertising hoardings on the right were the market gardens known as The Vineyard; the Winter Gardens were opened on their site on 25 March 1935 (see page 7). Immediately beyond The Vineyard is the Llandudno Museum and then the Gloddeath United Church, built in 1891; its present congregation was formed by the union of the local English Presbyterian and the United Reformed congregations. The building on the left with the dome, built in 1905, was the Seilo Welsh Presbyterian Church and is now the United Welsh Church of Llandudno. In this picture one of the original trams of 1907 is approaching down the middle of the road, heading towards the West Shore whilst in the background *La Marguerite* is steaming away from the pier on her way back to Liverpool.

Text © Bernard Byrom, 2012.
First published in the United Kingdom, 2012,
by Stenlake Publishing Ltd.
Telephone: 01290 551122
www.stenlake.co.uk

ISBN 9781840335873

**The publishers regret that they cannot supply
copies of any pictures featured in this book.**

Acknowledgements

The author wishes to thank the staff of Llandudno Library for their assistance during his research for this book.

The publishers wish to thank the following for permission to reproduce photographs in this book: R. Wiseman for the back cover; A.D. Parker for pages 7, 8, 14, 15 and 35; and Richard Casserley for page 54.

All attempts have been made to trace photographers of other tram photographs in this book. Please contact Stenlake Publishing if you have further information.

The books and websites listed below were used by the author during his research:

Christopher Draper & John Lawson-Reay, *Llandudno Through Time*, 2010
Ivor Wynne Jones, *Llandudno Queen of Welsh Resorts*, 2002
Stephen Lockwood, *Llandudno & Colwyn Bay Tramway*, 2007
Jim Roberts, *Llandudno Past and Present*, 2002
Jim Roberts, *Britain in Old Photographs – Llandudno*, 2009
Great Orme Tramway website
Journal of the Great Orme Exploration Society website
The Llandudno and Colwyn Bay Tramway Society website

Introduction

The popular North Wales holiday resort of Llandudno is situated in a sandy bay between the two headlands of the Great Orme and the Little Orme. Great Orme's Head is Llandudno's most distinctive feature. Connected to the mainland by the low-lying shelf of land on which Llandudno is built, it is a mile wide, stretches out into the sea for two miles and at its highest point is 679 feet above sea level. The Little Orme is two and half miles distant from her bigger neighbour across the bay and has a headland 463 feet above sea level. The Welsh name for the Great Orme is Gogarth and from its summit of Pen-y-Gogarth it is possible on a clear day to see the Isle of Man and even Ireland.

The area has a long history of human habitation, which is believed to go back as far as 12,000 years, and Bronze Age copper mines and various ancient artefacts have been discovered in the vicinity. The Romans came and extracted copper and lead whilst later miners quarried limestone. *A Topographical Dictionary of Wales*, published in 1849, mentions two copper mines on the Great Orme that between them produced about 3,000 tons of copper ore of a very pure quality and employed around 300 men. There were other mines besides these, but copper mining in Britain was already in decline by the late 1840s and the last three mines closed between 1856 and 1863.

In the middle of the nineteenth century Llandudno was merely a cluster of cottages and huts in and around the shoulder of the Great Orme with a population of approximately 1,000 who earned a precarious living from fishing, mining and farming. The town owes its present origins principally to three men: Edward Mostyn, MP for Flintshire, the Rt Revd Christopher Bethel, Lord Bishop of Bangor, and Owen Williams, a Liverpool architect. At a time when landlords all over Britain were using Acts of Parliament to enclose common land that had been used by villagers from time immemorial, the first two gentlemen colluded to enclose 955 acres of land where the town now stands. They achieved this by virtue of the Eglwysrhos, Llandudno and Llangystenin Enclosure Bill which passed into law in 1843 and left the villagers with a meagre 30 square yards in which to sink a communal well. Even today most of the land in the area is owned by the Mostyn Estates who have always exercised a great deal of control over the development of the town. The third man, Owen Williams, had visited the area and was impressed with its potential for becoming a resort; in 1844 he was introduced to Edward Mostyn who instructed him to make a survey and draw up plans for the development of the town. The editor of the *Liverpool Mercury* had already visited the small fishing village and enthused about it in the paper so much that visitors were already beginning to arrive by boat and facilities were needed to service them. The first 176 lots of land on prime sites were auctioned off in 1849 on 75-year leases for as little as 6d per square yard. At first there were very few bidders but then interest in the town's potential suddenly blossomed and was followed by rapid development.

By order of the Llandudno Improvement Act of 1854 a body of twenty Commissioners under the chairmanship of Lord Mostyn was set up to oversee the town's orderly development with wide main streets and quality buildings. By 1854 Mostyn Street and the Church Walk area were almost complete and the seafront hotels followed soon afterwards. The North Parade is the oldest part of the Promenade, the houses and hotels starting to appear in 1855 as the Promenade developed to meet St George's Hotel. The Queen's Hotel was built the following year and in the 1870s the town's development moved slowly across the bay towards the Little Orme and the Craig-y-Don area. In 1881 the population was 4,838 with an estimated 20,000 visitors during the summer. The West Shore and the Penrhyn Bay suburb were developed later than the other parts of the town, mainly after 1900. By then the Promenade extended the whole length of the bay; it is 90 feet wide and about a mile and a half long with seats and shelters along the whole length.

Early visitors to the town were mainly from the middle and professional classes but the coming of the railway meant that a wider social range from a wider area was able enjoy a seaside holiday. By 1936 the working week had been reduced to 48 hours from 54 and the Holidays with Pay Act of 1938 meant that working class families could now afford to take a week's seaside holiday. Along with the Lancashire coast resorts the North Wales coastal towns of Prestatyn, Rhyl, Colwyn Bay and Llandudno were the favourite destinations of workers from the industrial towns of the Midlands and northwest England throughout the 1950s and well into the 1960s, until the advent of affordable flights tempted them to warmer resorts abroad. Similarly, until family motorcars became more affordable, families almost invariably came by rail. On summer Saturdays there was a constant stream of trains heading to and from the North Wales resorts and as they all needed to pass through the bottleneck of Chester Station the horrendous delays along the line became legendary. But Llandudno thrived on it. The town's centenary brochure, published in 1954, claimed that there were around 2,000 hotels and boarding houses in the town that could accommodate 60,000 visitors a week between them. There were first class resident shows at the Pier Pavilion, the Arcadia and the Grand Theatre whilst Sunday concerts featuring famous stars were held at the Pier Pavilion. The town also boasted three cinemas, two ballrooms, an open-air concert party, the Pierhead Orchestra and the Town Band as well as a variety of outdoor sporting facilities. In recent years the building of the A55 link with the M6 and other major motorways has meant a decrease in the number of people staying in the resort and an increase in the number of day-trippers and short-stay visitors.

But things might have been so different! In 1853 the St George's Harbour and Railway Company had been given Parliamentary approval to turn the village of Llandudno into the main port of North Wales. Its promoters envisaged that, amongst other business, it would handle the export of coal from the Denbighshire coalfield and the town would be named Port Wrexham. The port's development would consist of 'breakwater, piers, jetties, lighthouses and other works for the safe and convenient passage of ships and other vessels into and out of port'. The waterfront would consist of 'walls, docks, slips, locks, reservoirs, quays, wharfs, moorings, staithes, drops, landing places and other buildings and works, together with a communication by railway to the port and its works'. A branch railway built from the Chester & Holyhead Railway would have run right through the present centre of town and terminated in the port in what is now Prince Edward Square. Work began with the pier being built in 1858 together with a three-mile branch line laid from Llandudno Junction. But nature took a hand in the shape of the Great Storm of 1859 which not only caused severe damage to the pier but showed that the bay was not sufficiently sheltered for the port that had been envisaged. So the whole project was abandoned and Llandudno was left in peace to continue developing into a fashionable watering place.

Steamer services along the North Wales coast have a long history, beginning in 1821 with the St George Steam Packet Company which was taken over by the City of Dublin Steam Packet Company in 1843. However, the major company that served the coast from 1891 to 1962 and which is still fondly remembered was the Liverpool and North Wales Steamship Company Ltd. After that time there were occasional visits from ships such as the *Waverley* and the *Balmoral* but in recent years the landing stage has become unsafe and no pleasure steamers now call at Llandudno.

The other main transport feature of the area was the 3 foot 6 inches gauge street tramway that ran from Llandudno to Colwyn Bay. It opened in 1907 and was extended to Old Colwyn in 1915, helping to accelerate the development of the district. It had a chequered history in its early days. The Llandudno and Colwyn Bay Light Railway Order of 1898 was accepted in 1899 by the Board of Trade and the construction of the line was scheduled but nothing happened for the next seven years of legal shilly-shallying and failed attempts to raise money. In 1904 the name of the company was changed to the Llandudno and Colwyn Bay Traction Co. Ltd but this alone did little to raise the necessary money. After repeated applications to the Board of Trade for time extensions, work eventually began on the line but with little discernable progress and in 1906 the company went into liquidation. This resulted in yet another name change to the Llandudno and District Electric Traction Construction Co. Ltd and from this point work at last gathered pace. By the end of July 1907 the section between West Parade Llandudno and Rhos-on-Sea was ready for operation and in 1909 there was a final name change to the Llandudno and Colwyn Bay Electric Railway Limited.

Originally there was a western terminus at Dale Street, Deganwy, from where the tramcars ran along West Parade to the tram shelter at West Shore where they turned sharp right to head into Llandudno. In practice the Deganwy section was very little used and so the trams soon began to terminate at the shelter and the Deganwy extension ceased to exist. The inaugural tram service officially ran from Sunday 19 October 1907 but religious proprieties had to be observed and services actually commenced the following day. A tramcar depot was built in Penrhyn Avenue, Rhos. Local controversies about route choice delayed the completion of the system from Rhos into Colwyn Bay which eventually opened on 7 June 1908 and in 1912 the company sought permission to continue the line into Old Colwyn to terminate at the Queen's Hotel near Penmaen Head. This section was completed and opened on 26 March 1915, which made the line nearly eight and a half miles long.

The route's tramcars were a mixed bag. Fourteen single-deck cars numbered 1 to 14 were purchased new from the Midland Carriage & Wagon Company of Shrewsbury for the opening of the line in 1907. They had capacity for 42 seated and 14 standing passengers and were built with two saloons, one for smoking and the other for non-smoking passengers. These were followed by four new four-wheeled semi-convertible cars, Nos. 15 to 18, which were built in Preston by the United Electric Car Co. Ltd and arrived in September 1909. These four cars could each carry 31 seated passengers and the staff called them 'Yankees' because of their foreign appearance. They were renowned for the squealing noise they made when going round tight corners, particularly when turning from Mostyn Street into Gloddaeth Street where the bend was so sharp that the squealing of the wheel flanges against the rails was likened by one councillor to 'the shrieking of Kilkenny cats' and led to many complaints by local residents and tradespeople. The tramway company's solution was to grease the rails! They were withdrawn in 1936 and stored until 1941 when their bodies were sold for sheds to the army camps of Rhyl and Bodelwyddan. In 1914 four open-deck 'Toastrack' cars were ordered from the United Electric Car Company (UEC) but wartime conditions delayed their building and they were finally delivered in 1920, by which time UEC had merged with English Electric. These had seating for 60 passengers on fourteen full-width liftover bench seats and two half-width liftover seats on either side of the trolley mast and they lasted almost until the end of services. Further additions to the fleet that appear in this book were five single-deck trams bought second-hand from Accrington Corporation in 1932 and ten double-deck trams with open top decks, bought second-hand from Bournemouth Corporation in 1936. The final acquisitions in 1946, not shown in this book, were two ten-year-old streamlined double-deck trams from Darwen Corporation which had a carrying capacity of 56 passengers. These had to be re-gauged down from Darwen's 4 foot gauge to Llandudno's 3 foot 6 inches gauge.

A contemporary description of the journey says: 'A country prospect presented itself to top-deck passengers as the tram left Mostyn Broadway, crossed Nant-y-Gamar Road and proceeded towards Craigside over the track cut through Bodafon Fields. There was the expectation of the climb up Penrhyn Hill and the rush down the Little Orme cutting into Penrhyn Bay'. This brought the trams down to the seafront at Rhos-on-Sea which is probably the oldest inhabited part of Colwyn Bay. It developed around the ancient church of Llandrillo-yn-Rhos which was a prominent landmark for sailors on the Irish Sea as they sailed to and from Liverpool. The promenade was extended from Colwyn Bay around 1909 and Rhos is nowadays a thriving community. Beyond Rhos the tramway continued into Colwyn Bay itself; this town's existence was the direct consequence of the death of Sir David Erskine who lived at Pwllycrochan and died in 1842 at the age of 48. He owned the majority of the land on which Colwyn Bay now stands and for 23 years after his death his widow and son carried on managing the estate. But by 1865 they could continue no longer and sold the land, with the result that within thirty years the new town of Colwyn Bay had sprung up. Wealthy people from Lancashire and Yorkshire began to settle in the area and families started to come for their holidays. Many who had holidayed here for years chose to make it their place of retirement and some former hotels and guest houses have been converted into retirement apartments or care homes. The original village, appropriately named Old Colwyn, developed around the Colwyn River. The main road used to run through the centres of both Old Colwyn and Colwyn Bay but the present A55, built in the 1980s, bypasses both places.

The trams were popular with holidaymakers for over half a century but in the early 1950s the company began to experience difficulties. There was a lack of investment in its infrastructure, particularly as the line was being subjected to fierce competition from the bus companies. Electricity supply was problematical, the popularity of the family car was making local transport increasingly unnecessary and the tramway was adding problems to road congestion. Their demise was inevitable and the last tram ran on the evening of 24 March 1956; their tramlines are now covered by the modern roadway. After closure of the tramway the company struggled on for a few more years using motorbuses, but in 1961 they bowed to the inevitable and sold their business to their main rivals, the Crosville Motor Company.

But Llandudno does have a tramway that is still thriving – the 3 foot 6 inches gauge Great Orme Tramway. At the end of the nineteenth century there were suggestions that a funicular (cable) railway might ease the passage to the top for tourists and goods. Under this type of operation a vehicle is permanently fixed to a cable laid between the rails. A consortium of local businessmen and well-to-do local residents made proposals for a tramway and in the winter of 1897/98 they promoted a Parliamentary bill for permission to build the line. It took two years for the legal and bureaucratic processes to be cleared before the scheme was given the go-ahead in October 1900. Contractors were appointed in April 1901 and work began but progress was slow. Eventually on 30 July 1902 the Board of Trade Inspector, Colonel von Donop, passed the lower section as fit for traffic and the Great Orme Tramways Company commenced services next day with the town band playing away the first tram with the National Anthem. The journey is in two parts because it is too long a distance for a single draw cable. The second section to the summit, on which the gradients were easier, was completed the following year

and opened on 8 July 1903. It is the longest funicular railway in Great Britain but has not been without its difficulties over the years. A bad accident in 1932 resulted in the company going into liquidation the following year. Sold in 1934 for £5,600 to a syndicate of former shareholders who changed its name to the Great Orme Railway Limited, the tramway continued operating until Llandudno UDC exercised its right in 1947 to buy the line, which it did for around £8,500. Following periodic local government reorganisations since that time its operation is currently the responsibility of Conwy County Borough Council. The system has been modernised over the past century but the four original cars used on the opening day in 1902 are still in operation today and carry thousands of holidaymakers to a panoramic view of Llandudno and its bay.

A Crosville-owned Bristol Lodekka bus and original tramcar No. 2 race each other down Bryn-y-Bia Road on Penrhynside in the direction of Llandudno in the early 1950s. Whichever one was first on this occasion, there was ultimately only one winner and that was the bus service.

An ex-Bournemouth tram, believed to be No. 11 built in 1921, passing the Odeon Cinema in Gloddaeth Street and leaving the end of the passing loop opposite Clifton Road on its way from West Shore to Mostyn Street in the early 1950s. The Winter Gardens complex was a theatre, cinema and dance hall built in 1934 by James and Zachary Brierley of Rochdale at a cost of £70,000. In December 1936 it was acquired by Odeon Theatres Ltd although it wasn't renamed 'Odeon' until 1943. The building may have become a cinema but the words 'Theatre Ballroom' were still inscribed in large letters above its entrance and 'Winter Gardens' high on the wall on its far side. In 1969 it was sold to the independent Hutchinson circuit who renamed it the Astra Cinema but it closed in October 1986 and the building was demolished in 1989, being replaced by residential accommodation named Ormside Grange. Nowadays cars park along the length of the road where the tall posts holding the tram wires appear in the picture.

Seen here in August 1949, original tramcar No. 18 has turned from Mostyn Street into Gloddaeth Street en route to the West Shore. This tramcar had been renumbered from No. 11 and lasted until the end of the service in 1956. The large white building is the Clarence Hotel, once a high-class hotel but nowadays closed and boarded up. The nearer building on the right houses the ladies fashion shop Marie et Cie. The building on the extreme left with the higher rooftop is the former Palladium Cinema that was built in 1920 but designed in Edwardian days, replacing an earlier market hall built in 1864. It is now a Wetherspoon's pub and thankfully its owners have restored its ornate interior and façade.

New Electric Tram. Llandudno.

Pictured on a very rainy and windswept day in 1907, soon after services began, original tramcar No. 3 swings round the corner from Mostyn Street into Gloddaeth Street and approaches George Street. A pawnbroker's shop is visible in Upper Mostyn Street, its traditional sign of three brass balls hanging from a bracket on the first floor.

The inland cliffs of the Great Orme make an impressive backdrop as original tramcar No. 11 takes the sharp turn at Hooson's Corner from Mostyn Street into Gloddaeth Street in the first year of operation. The large grocery shop on the corner belonged to T. Esmor Hooson whose business had been established since 1854 and who gave his name to the corner. This location is nowadays known as the Palladium Corner.

This tramcar is one of the five purchased second-hand from Accrington Corporation Tramways in 1932 to replace five of the original ones of 1907, which were then scrapped. They came into service in 1933 and three of them, including this one, received trucks from three of the scrapped tramcars; the other two had to be re-gauged from the Accrington 4-foot gauge. This one received old No. 4's truck. They had wooden seats until 1950 when they were upholstered with cushions from former Birmingham trams. This 1934 photograph shows the tram about to turn the corner from Gloddaeth Street into Mostyn Street with the Carlton Hotel prominent on the corner and Woolworth's shop visible in Mostyn Street. The buildings beyond the Carlton are hotels in South Parade which leads down to the seafront.

Mostyn Street, Llandudno, c.32

Original tramcar No. 6 waits for a tardy pony and cart to clear the tracks before turning from Mostyn Street into Gloddaeth Street; an oncoming tramcar waits to make the turn in the opposite direction. The pony and cart belonged to the town crier who also conducted business as a porter. A line of horse-drawn cabs is standing in the middle of the roadway beyond the junction, waiting for shoppers' custom. The Carlton Buffet and Bar is on the right of the picture next to the shops of Stange & Co. (greengrocers and florists) and Briggs & Co. of Leicester (boot and shoe makers).

23418. Mostyn Street, Llandudno.

The view from the top of Hooson's shop, looking down Mostyn Street from its junction with Gloddaeth Street on the right. Mostyn Street was the most elegant street in the town and, indeed, in North Wales. Its wide roadway gave ample space for both tramcars and other vehicles and its wide pavements had verandas to protect shoppers from inclement weather. The buildings themselves were generally very stylish, a tribute to the strict building controls exercised by the Improvement Commissioners. The posts topped with a circle denote tramcar boarding stops; the tramway itself was generally single track through the town with passing loops at intervals, as can be seen here.

Tramcar No. 6, seen here in the 1950s heading into Llandudno down Mostyn Street and past the Alexandra Hotel on the corner of Clonmel Street and opposite Trinity Square. This tramcar, ex-Bournemouth Corporation Tramways and built in 1914, has since been saved for preservation and is on display at the Electricity Museum in Christchurch, Dorset, painted in its original Bournemouth livery and with its original number 85. The large white building in the background is the Tudno Castle Hotel, formerly the North Western Hotel which had been built by the London & North Western Railway Company as its prestige hotel in the town. In 2008 the hotel was closed and permission was granted for the main part of the building to be demolished and redeveloped provided that the facades were preserved. Unfortunately this scheme ran into financial difficulties and at the present time the hotel is standing empty. Like many trams pictured in this book this one is advertising Catlin Follies. Will Catlin (1872–1953) came to Llandudno in 1915 after building a show business empire in Scarborough and purchased the near-derelict Hippodrome Skating Rink on the promenade for £400, refurbished it and renamed it the Arcadia. He styled himself the 'Great Showman' and introduced a troupe of pierrots which he later named the 'Catlin Follies'. The Follies survived his death in 1953 and continued until the theatre was bought by the local council in 1968, after which it continued as a summer theatre until 1993. It was then closed and lay derelict until being demolished in 2005 to make way for the present Venue Cymru theatre, conference centre and arena.

Ex-Bournemouth tramcar No. 11, built in 1921, is here approaching the town centre from Mostyn Avenue into the beginning of Mostyn Broadway at the junction with Queen's Road. In this photograph, taken on the last day of the tramway's service on 24 March 1956, passengers are boarding the tram whilst a man in the roadway appears to be asking the driver for directions. The roadway itself appears to have been patched up in several places, most noticeably across the adjoining track. Further down the road the tramway's nemesis – a bus – is taking passengers for Colwyn Bay. The large millinery shop on the right is Mrs Mackay's who traded as 'Adrian' and the bank across the road is the National Provincial, nowadays part of the NatWest Banking Group. The veranda is still in place but the bank is no longer there. The motor car entering from the right is one of the Triumph 'Renown' models that were known as 'Razor Edge' because of their angular bodywork.

The Pier Pavilion of 1886 is prominent in the centre of this 1904 photograph and, next to it, the Grand Hotel is in the process of being constructed. Bathing machines were introduced into Llandudno in 1855 and although there is only one visible in this picture there was usually a whole line of them stretched out along the seashore. Nude bathing was popular in Victorian times and the bathing machines were horse-drawn into the water until it was deep enough to prevent 'indecent exposure' of their occupants. So far as bathing on the beach was concerned the sexes were segregated, women and children bathing in one part of the beach and gentlemen in another; there was a 200-yard gap between the two areas. Mixed bathing wasn't allowed until 1894 and then only on one part of the beach opposite the Arcadia Theatre. Incredibly, these bathing machines lasted at Llandudno until 1958. Bath chairs used to be in great demand for the less able-bodied. Some were made of wickerwork and some were coach-built with half folding doors across the front to keep the wind off the occupant. They had three wheels and could be hired by the hour or by the day, being either pushed or pulled by a hired attendant (if one was required) with the occupant steering. They lasted until the First World War.

Edwardian holidaymakers pictured enjoying a day on the sands in the sunshine. The tower of St George's Hotel, built in 1854 and owned at the outset by 24-year-old Isaiah Davies, is easily recognisable behind them on the North Parade. Most of the people seen here are from the middle and upper middle classes but look at their beach clothes compared with today's outfits!

PAVILION, GRAND HOTEL AND BEACH, LLANDUDNO.

The Grand Hotel dates from 1901 and was relatively newly built when this Edwardian photograph was taken. The hotel had 156 bedrooms and was for many years the largest hotel in Wales. Previously the town's Baths, Reading Room and Billiard Hall had stood on the site; built in 1855, they were demolished to make way for the hotel. The Pier Pavilion was opened in 1886 and originally had a glass roof but stormy weather soon necessitated its rebuilding. In 1887 Jules Riviere had been engaged to conduct the seven-piece Tylor's Band at the end of the pier but he saw the opportunities offered by the newly built Pavilion and after initial opposition he moved in. It was well known for its orchestral concerts which attracted celebrity artistes; Sir Malcolm Sargent was the orchestra's conductor for two seasons in 1926–1928, Sir Adrian Boult was a guest conductor on several occasions and Adelina Patti also appeared. But by 1994 the Pavilion was unused and slowly disintegrating under the battering of the weather. It was totally destroyed by fire in February that year and since then the site has stood empty, a derelict eyesore with its decorative ironwork now pointing forlornly into empty space.

Llandudno's first pier, constructed in 1858, was only 242 feet long and built on sixteen wooden piles. The great storm of October 1859, which caused the loss of 223 vessels and 800 lives around the British Isles, severely damaged the pier and although it was repaired and lasted for a further sixteen years it was too short for pleasure steamers which were becoming larger in size and which could only use it at high tide. The present pier, pictured here around 1916 when the admission price was 2*d*, opened on 1 August 1877 and an additional landwards spur was added to it in 1884. Nowadays a Grade II listed structure, it was designed by Charles Henry Driver in conjunction with the eminent engineer Sir James Brunlees who had already constructed the piers at Rhyl and Southport. At 2,295 feet long it needed to be both tall and light to cope with the strong currents below. There is a great deal of ornamental ironwork in the railings, lampposts and brackets, and it is one of the best preserved of Britain's surviving cast-iron piers with its long promenade, T-shaped landing stage and sequence of small kiosks like miniature pagodas. In the background of this view the twin-funnelled *La Marguerite* has reversed away from the pier landing stage to allow another pleasure steamer to berth.

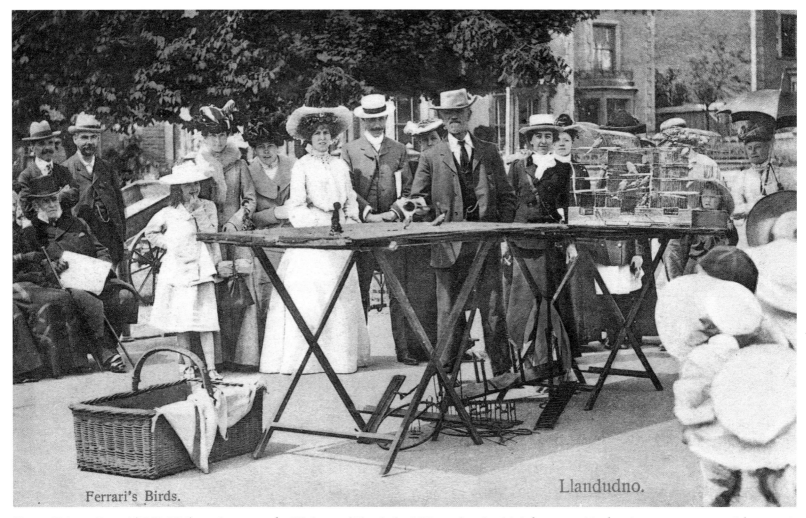

Ferrari's Birds.

Llandudno.

Signor Gicianto Ferrari (1847–1923) was known as the 'Birdman of Llandudno'. His performing bird shows outside the pier gates were one of the resort's most popular attractions for many years and, as this early Edwardian picture shows, attracted an audience of all ages. His budgies and canaries were trained to perform a variety of tricks including pulling tiny coaches complete with passengers, walking on tightropes, flying round the Grand Hotel and back, swinging on a trapeze and even firing a small cannon.

Massey Series

Llandudno Pier & Jetty

The big attraction for these holidaymakers one week in the late 1920s was a two-shilling sail around the battleship HMS *Iron Duke*, which was on a courtesy visit to the town. The *Iron Duke* had been built at Portsmouth between 1912 and 1914 at the staggering cost (for those days) of nearly £2 million. Named after the Duke of Wellington, she became the flagship of the Grand Fleet under Admiral Sir John Jellicoe and was involved in the Battle of Jutland in 1916. After the war she served in the Mediterranean fleet as Sir John de Robeck's flagship and subsequently in the Atlantic fleet until she was paid off in 1929. Her next task was as a gunnery training vessel until the outbreak of the Second World War when she was moved to Scapa Flow as a base vessel. Here she survived damage from German bombing raids but after the conclusion of hostilities she was sold for scrap in 1946 and was broken up in Glasgow in 1948. The pleasure launch at the jetty is *White Thistle* who, with her sister ship *White Heather*, ran trips around the local coastline.

The pleasure steamer *La Marguerite*, seen here in 1905, was built in 1894 by Fairfield Shipbuilding & Engineering Company of Govan and operated by Palace Steamers on a cross-channel service from Tilbury and Margate to Boulogne, later extended two days a week to Ostend and also to Calais. All these operations proved unprofitable and she was sold to the Liverpool & North Wales Steamship Company in 1904. She had a gross tonnage of 1,554 tons, was 342 feet in length and could carry over 2,000 passengers when full. She was easily the most popular ship on the Liverpool–Llandudno–Menai Straits route and there were days when she carried as many as 1,000 day-trippers into Llandudno. During the First World War she was used as a troopship across the Channel before returning to her pre-war work. To the sorrow of thousands of her admirers, her last voyage was on 28 September 1925 and she was broken up at Briton Ferry in 1926.

The *Greyhound* was the finest of the limited number of steamers based in Blackpool. She was built in 1895 for the North Pier Steamship Company and passed to the Blackpool Passenger Steamboat Company after about ten years. She operated services from Blackpool to Llandudno and Douglas but on Sundays she sailed from Liverpool to Blackpool. Seen here off Llandudno's pier head in 1905, she returned to Blackpool after the First World War but was found to be no longer profitable in service and was sold to owners in Belfast in 1923. Following a boiler accident in 1924 she was sold for service in Turkey and renamed *Buyukada*.

For the 1926 season *La Marguerite* was replaced by *St Tudno III* which was joined in 1931 by the latter's smaller sister ship, the *St Seiriol II*, pictured here, which was named after a local sixth century saint. She was built at Fairfield's yard in Govan and launched on 5 March 1931. In the 1920s fares from Liverpool to Llandudno had been 7/- for the First Class Saloon and 5/- for the Second Class Saloon for the round trip, leaving daily at 10.45 a.m. and arriving back at 7.30 p.m. and with four hours ashore at Llandudno. The voyage continued to Menai Bridge (2/- extra) or completed a round trip of Anglesey for a further 2/-. Dinners at 4/- and afternoon teas at 3/- were served in the First Class Dining Saloon. By the mid 1930s the first class fare to Llandudno had increased to 8/- and second class to 6/-. In the Second World War *St Seiriol II* played a significant part in the evacuation of Dunkirk, returning to the beach seven times and suffering only superficial damage. Here she is seen passing Great Orme's Head on her way from Llandudno to Menai Bridge. The excursion service came to an end in 1962 and she was broken up in Ghent in the following year.

A little way from the pier is a former limestone quarry whose shape formed a natural amphitheatre. To commemorate Queen Victoria's Golden Jubilee in 1887 Lord Mostyn presented it to the town as a place for large-scale outdoor entertainment, calling it the Happy Valley. He himself carried out the opening ceremony and in August 1890 his mother presented a canopied drinking fountain with a bronze bust of Queen Victoria. This view of the crowds at Happy Valley dates from the beginning of the twentieth century. During performances the better-off audiences would sit in deckchairs at a few pence a time but the majority watched for nothing from the hillside, melting away into the distance whenever a man with a collecting box appeared. In complete contrast to the entertainment, fervent nonconformist and evangelical meetings were held here on Sundays.

The Happy Valley was the place to go for entertainment. This view is looking in the opposite direction to the previous picture, towards the Marine Drive and the Great Orme. The earliest entertainers in the valley were a husband and wife team who used a tent as a changing room. Churchill's Minstrels entertained the crowds here for many years before the outbreak of the First World War, Billy Churchill appearing before the king and queen in the first Royal Command Performance at London's Palace Theatre in 1912. Another popular group that entertained the crowds in the inter-war years was the Charles Wade Concord Follies.

COLONNADES, HAPPY VALLEY, LLANDUDNO. 8899.

Lord Mostyn opened this impressive stone colonnade leading from the promenade to Happy Valley on 31 March 1932. Designed by G.A. Humpreys of Mostyn Estates and built by W.T. Ward, it is 185 yards long, fourteen feet wide and cost £6,500.

An early twentieth century view from Happy Valley of the tollhouse at the entrance to the Marine Drive. The canopied drinking fountain with a bronze bust of Queen Victoria, which was presented by Lady Mostyn, can be seen on the left of the picture. Before the Marine Drive was built there was only a footpath around the Great Orme and this was known as Cust's Path after a lawyer of that name who was also a Mostyn Estates trustee. He instigated the building of the path between 1856 and 1858 but it was very dangerous with precipitous drops to the sea below. No railings were provided and it is said that when Prime Minister William Gladstone came in 1868 to visit his friend Dean Liddell, who had a house nearby on the West Shore, he had to be blindfolded and led by hand along the more frightening stretches of the path. Many thousands of tons of rock had to be removed to provide a level surface for the subsequent road and a number of megalithic tombs were destroyed in the process.

The Lido bathing pool was built at Deganwy on the west shore of the Great Orme and near the western end of the Marine Drive. It opened in August 1934 and in addition to a large swimming pool of filtered seawater there was a special pool for diving with water chutes for the children. Facilities included a restaurant with dancing and concert facilities and even a small zoo. 8,000 spectators could watch 1,000 swimmers but the numbers in this late-1930s picture appear to be considerably less than capacity! With post-war patronage dwindling the Lido closed in the 1950s and was replaced by a housing estate in 1963.

LITTLE ORME, LLANDUDNO.

The Little Orme headland stands at the eastern end of Llandudno Bay and these Victorian promenaders are walking along what is now Colwyn Road. The building behind the horse-drawn coach is the Craigside Hydropathic Establishment, which was built in 1888 but demolished in 1974. Its indoor tennis courts were situated on the other side of the road.

Returning to the eastwards route of the tramway, Llandudno-bound original tramcar No. 3 has left the shelf at the top of the climb up from Penrhyn Bay and is now descending the incline at the top of Bryn-y-Bia Road before heading through the Bodavon fields towards Mostyn Avenue. The photograph was taken in the very early days of the tramway and the tramcar has only one trolley (they were soon replaced with a double pole) and is painted 'Llandudno & Colwyn Bay'; its livery was maroon and cream. The large house on the right is Sunny Hill which was built in 1887 for Joseph Broome, a wealthy Manchester cotton trader. After his death in 1907 the house was taken over by Arnhall Girls School in 1913 and after they moved out in 1935 it became a Dr Barnardo's Home for Girls from 1949 until 1981. A series of short-term tenancies followed until eventually the house was demolished in 2008 and its site redeveloped for modern housing.

Tramway Car, Penrhyn Hill, Nr Llandudno.

Original tramcar No. 14, pictured at the top of Bryn-y-Bia Road, and about to descend Penrhyn Hill on its way to Colwyn Bay, soon after the service began. The signpost indicates that the road to Bodafon Road runs out of the bottom of the picture and Colwyn Road curves away to the left with Pendre Road going off to the right.

PENRHYNSIDE

225/47

The village of Penrhynside clings to the slopes of Penrhyn Hill above Penrhyn Old Hall. It was originally a quarry workers' village, the men working in the limestone quarry on the Little Orme from 1889 until production ceased in 1931. In this 1933 photograph one of the original tramcars of 1907 is heading for Llandudno up Penrhyn Hill in the direction of Bryn-y-Bia Road.

P.C. 41738 Llandudno & Colwyn Bay Tramway Penrhyn Hill Cutting & Rhos.

A panoramic view over Rhos and round Colwyn Bay as another of the original 1907 tramcars climbs through the cutting on Penrhyn Hill on its way to Llandudno. The shelf was blasted into the side of the Little Orme to ease the steepness of the gradient. Penrhyn Old Hall farm outbuildings are on the right and Rhos is in the background. At the foot of the hill the tramway turns left along Glan y Mor Road towards the seafront whilst the road snaking through the middle of the picture is Penrhyn Isaf Road.

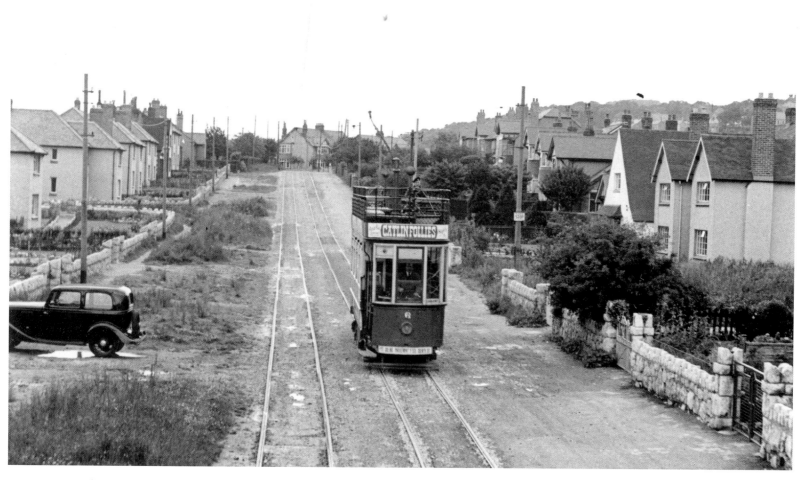

Ex-Bournemouth tramcar No. 6, built in 1914, runs down Glan y Mor Road on its way to Colwyn Bay after passing the junction with Penrhyn Isaf Road on the bend at St David's Corner at the top of the hill. At this time of this photograph, taken in the 1950s, Glan y Mor Road was owned by the tramway company and was in a rather poor condition, being both unadopted by the local authority and unsurfaced. In 1963 the local authority purchased the road and surfaced it in the following year.

With the Little Orme on the right, a 'Toastrack' tramcar begins its run on the seafront at Penrhyn Bay along Marine Drive (now part of Glan y Mor Road) towards Rhos-on-Sea on its way to Colwyn Bay in July 1953. The track on the right has been abandoned because of gale damage the previous year. These cars were extremely popular with tourists and a ride on one down the Little Orme cutting was said to be particularly exhilarating! All four were taken out of service at the end of the summer season in September 1955.

Two ex-Bournemouth tramcars are passing on the reserved section of track on the seashore further along Penrhyn Bay near Maesgwyn Road. In this picture the original latticed posts for the tramlines are still in use; these were later replaced by the single but more solid posts seen in the previous picture.

A forlorn scene in a wintry Penryn Bay as ex-Accrington tramcar No. 3 heads along Marine Drive towards Glan y Mor Road en route to Llandudno on the last day of the tramway's operation on 24 March 1956. The seaward track that was badly damaged and undermined in the gales of 1952 was never reinstated; this section of the track was abandoned and single-line working (see also page 36) was instituted on the landward track until the tramway's closure. The terraced houses on the right were known as Quarry Cottages because they originally housed workers from the nearby quarry on the Little Orme.

Ex-Bournemouth tramcar No. 15, built in 1925, pictured in 1951 being chased along Penrhyn Avenue by a Crosville bus as they both head for Colwyn Bay. The tramway company bought land in 1907 to extend the track from Penrhyn Bay to Rhos and the present-day Penrhyn Avenue was once known as Tramway Avenue.

Pictured in 1951, two ex-Accrington tramcars (No. 5 on the left) are standing outside the tram depot that was built in Penrhyn Avenue in 1907 to provide covered accommodation for the initial fourteen tramcars and provide repair facilities in an eight-lane terminus. The site covered about one and a quarter acres of land in an area known locally as the Klondyke because at that time it was in the 'back of beyond'. The building survived until 2006, when it was demolished, and the site was redeveloped for housing.

On the seafront at Rhos-on-Sea original tramcar No. 1 has just passed the Cayley Arms and the junction with Rhos Road on its way to Llandudno. Rhos Pier in the background was 1,240 yards long; it was constructed in 1896 but was closed during the Second World War and much of the decking was removed by the local Home Guard to hinder any invading force. In happier times steamers used to sail from here to Liverpool and Anglesey, but following years of neglect the pier was demolished with explosives in April 1954.

Upper Promenade, Rhos on Sea

5641

Ex-Bournemouth tramcar No. 15, built in 1925, has left Rhos promenade and is climbing Whitehall Road towards Colwyn Bay. The nearest building on the left is the Mount Stewart Hotel.

Ex-Accrington tramcar No. 2, seen here in the 1950s passing Harrison's plumbers and ironmongers shop in Conway Road, Colwyn Bay, on its way to its then terminus at Aston's Corner at the top of Greenfield Road.

Ex-Bournemouth tramcar No. 6 was built in 1914 by the United Electric Car Company (the remainder of the Bournemouth tramcars were built by the Brush Company of Loughborough) and seen here on 24 August 1953 passing the former Congregational church in Colwyn Bay's Abergele Road on the final part of its journey from Llandudno. This church has an interesting history because it was the result of a joint effort of Welsh and English Congregationalist pioneers who bought the land in 1874. They erected a church (Antioch) and held services in both languages but the arrangement proved unsatisfactory and in 1882 the English formed a separate church although both congregations continued to use the same building. Eventually the English bought the Welsh church's share of the ground and commissioned Owen Edwards of Rhyl to design this gothic-style building, which was opened in 1885. Subsequently, in 1946, the English Baptists united with the Congregationalists and the building became known as the Union Church but in recent years it has been closed. Planning permission was granted by Conwy County Borough Council for a change of use from a church to a dance and arts centre and the building was put up for sale in 2011.

Ex-Bournemouth tramcar No. 10, pictured in 1951 as it stands at the Colwyn Bay terminus in Abergele Road with the conductor in the process of changing the trolley pole round for the return journey to Llandudno. This tramcar was built in 1921 and scrapped in January 1956. Minton's shop, selling wallpapers, paints and distempers, is on the right of the picture with the sunblind and Rhiw Bank Avenue runs off on the left.

Another view of tramcar No. 10 at the terminus in Abergele Road, this time looking in the opposite direction to the previous picture and with Greenfield Road on the left. The building on the facing left-hand corner had a large round tower at this time but the tower later became unsafe and was demolished in the 1960s. Nowadays the glass-topped verandas along the pavement have also gone. The visible shops are Jenkinson & Sons, seedsmen, E. Rowley, draper, and Abel Jones, fruiterer.

This original tramcar, pictured in the 1920s, is running along Abergele Road on the extension to the Queen's Hotel at Old Colwyn which opened in 1915. This was the first section of the route to disappear in 1930 when it was taken over by local bus services. The white cottages on the right were known as Plough Terrace and have since been demolished. The Plough Hotel itself on the right still stands today, but the one-time terminus of the Queen's Hotel further down Abergele Road has closed as a hotel and is now an Acorn Activity Centre providing specialist day care for patients with learning disabilities and mental health disorders. The road running to the left out of the picture is Berthes Road.

Abergele Road, Old Colwyn.

A scene in Abergele Road around 1918. This was the former turnpike road which was constructed a few years before Telford's survey of 1811 and which he described as 'The Present Mail Road'. Treleaven's Prize Bakery is at the far end of the row on the left, at its junction with Princess Road. The bank on the left, which is on the corner of Cefn Road, is a branch of the London City & Midland Bank, which was formed when the Birmingham & Midland Bank merged with the Central Bank of London Limited in 1891 and then with the City Bank in 1898. It adopted the shorter title of Midland Bank in 1923. The building is nowadays a pharmacy and the shops beyond it are still there but have lost their verandas. The porch of the Ship Hotel is on the right of the picture but it closed its doors to customers after Christmas 2010. The tramcar in centre of the picture is of the original 1907 batch and is descending from the Old Colwyn terminus towards Llandudno.

Seen here in the summer of 1923, away from the trams and the bustle of Colwyn Bay town centre, a young mother (or nanny) has crossed the promenade and is heading for the seashore with an eager-looking small boy in her pram. On the left a man is selecting a penny chocolate bar from a slot machine. Note the serpents' head decorative supports for the promenade seat. The building behind them is now The Toad pub and restaurant; the building next to it has been replaced with a modern building but its neighbour still stands on the corner of Sea Bank Road.

Unlike the late and much lamented Llandudno & Colwyn Bay Tramway featured in the previous pages, the Great Orme Tramway is still very much alive and flourishing. Construction of this 3 feet 6 inch gauge line began in 1901 and it opened from a terminus in Church Walks, Llandudno, on 31 July 1902. The terminus was subsequently realigned and enlarged, necessitating the demolition of the adjacent Victoria Hotel after which the terminus is named. In this picture tramcar No. 4 is seen in the station on 3 October 1966.

Seen here in the 1950s, these passengers on tramcar No. 5 have a panoramic view over Llandudno Bay as it climbs alongside the very steep Ty Gwyn Road just by its junction with Tyn-y-Coed Road on the lower section of the line. The gradient here is generally 1 in 4 (25%) with one stretch as steep as 1 in 3.6. Each one of the four double-bogie cars on the tramway is 37 feet long and accommodates 48 passengers on wooden seats.

Having just passed the location of the previous picture on its way uphill, tramcar No. 5 has now made a photographic stop, to its passengers' obvious delight.

GREAT ORME TRAM, LLANDUDNO.

Tramcar No. 4, pictured in 1938 descending Ty Gwyn Road towards the five-way road junction at Black Gate where an ascending car has stopped. Traffic lights were installed at this dangerous junction in 1992 with special signals for the tramway linked to sensors under the track. The reason that the cars have trolley poles when they are actually hauled by a rope laid between the tracks is that the trolley was used solely to maintain a telegraph link with the control unit at the halfway winding house. A second crewmember always had to travel on every tramcar's rear platform in case the trolley became detached from its copper wire and he had to restore communication quickly. This system lasted until the 1990s when radio control was introduced on the tramway and double-manning of the tram became unnecessary.

The halfway station is 489 feet above sea level and in this view from 12 August 1953 summer holidaymakers are climbing aboard tramcar No. 5 for the downhill journey back to the town. The reason for the journey being in two parts is because it is too long a distance for a single draw cable. When the tramway first opened, the power for the engine room and winding house was provided by a locomotive-type coke-fired boiler but this was replaced by a larger second-hand boiler in the 1920s and finally by the conversion to electricity in 1957. A substantial new winding house and station buildings were constructed in 2000/01.

65037   The Great Orme Tram, LLandudno.   JW.

The top section of the line opened on 8 July 1903 and here two tramcars are passing in the midway loop on this upper section in the early years of its operation. The halfway house is in the background with steam rising from its engine house boilers. These used to burn around 8,250 tons of coke a year to provide steam to power the system until it changed over to electricity.

The summit of the Great Orme has played an important part in communications over the years. A semaphore station was built here in 1826 by the Liverpool Docks' trustees and was part of a linked system which stretched from Liverpool to Holyhead. Messages were relayed visually by a series of moving arms but this, of course, could only be used in daylight. The station was rebuilt in 1841 but in 1861 the system was replaced by electric telegraph and the station was incorporated into the Telegraph Inn built on the summit. In 1909 the inn was replaced by the new hotel seen here which had an adjoining eighteen-hole golf course. Unfortunately, the project ran into financial difficulties even whilst it was under way; the hotel was completed on a less ambitious scale than planned and a local club was formed to complete and operate the golf club. During the Second World War the hotel was requisitioned by the Royal Air Force and became the Great Orme Radar Station. The golf course, which had never been very popular because of the high winds that often swept across the Great Orme, was subsequently sold to a local farmer and reverted to sheep pasture. In 1952 the ex-Middleweight boxing champion Randolph Turpin, together with associates, bought the hotel for £10,000. They renovated and modernised it, the opening ceremony being conducted by the ex-World Flyweight Champion Jimmy Wilde. Six years later Turpin became the sole licensee until 1961 when he ran into financial difficulties with the Inland Revenue and sold the hotel to Llandudno Council; he subsequently committed suicide in 1966 at the age of 37. Over the years the Summit Complex, as it is now called, has been extensively enlarged and includes a bar, restaurant and children's play area. The tramway passengers didn't have any shelter here at all until 1965 when a small brick-built building was provided; the present station and visitor centre date from 1992.